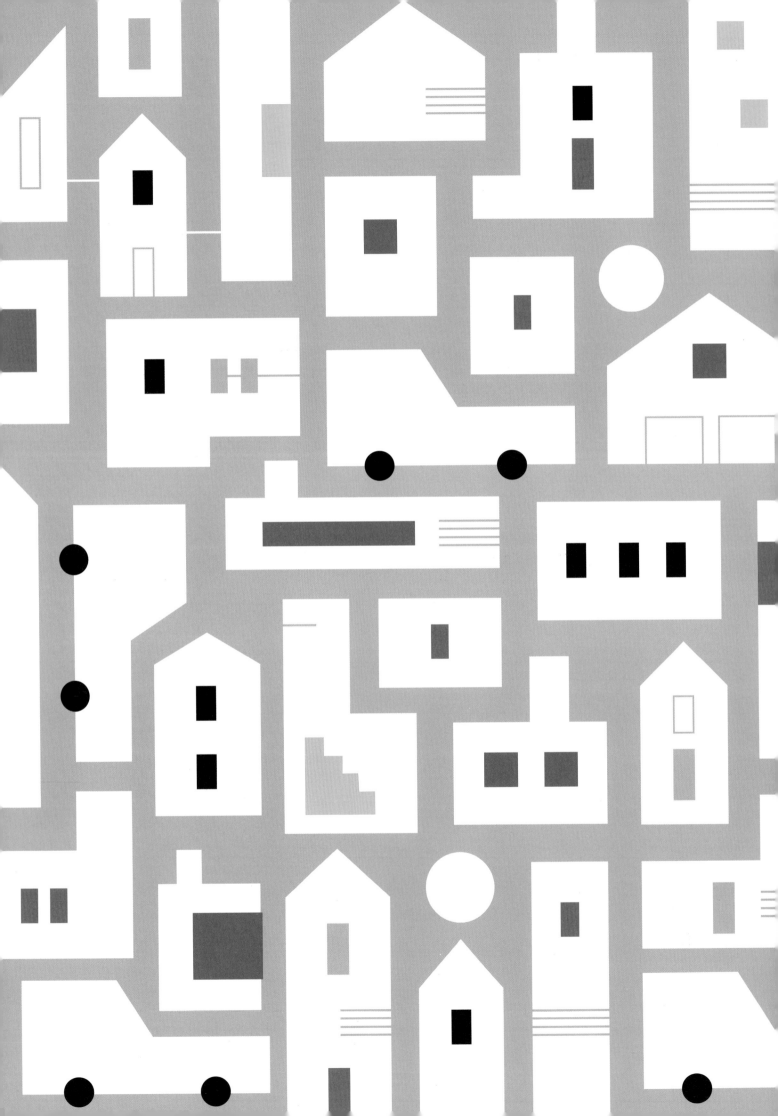

In The City

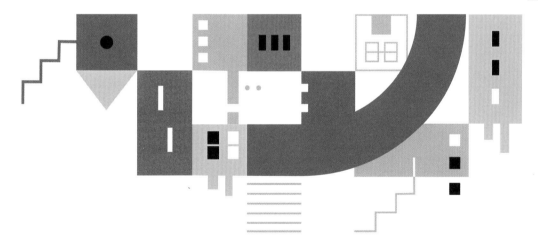

Dominika Lipniewska

Button
BOOKS

The city wakes up slowly.

Soon everything
moves very fast

in the hustle and bustle
of the morning rush.

In the
city, you
can find
buildings
that are tall

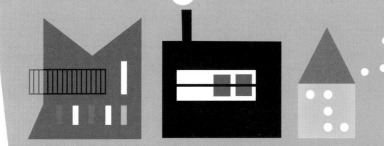

and some that
are small.

There are places to go that are green and leafy where you can find creatures of all sizes.

How many can you spot?

The people are all very different

but they often like the same things.

The city can be a very noisy place.

What a lot of sounds! Which one do you think is the loudest?

Luckily, you can always find a
quiet place to sit, rest, and eat.

There are also places where you can play!

In the city, people travel around in different ways.

Which vehicles
have you been in?

There are always new tastes
and smells to discover

and you can eat different
types of food every day.

You can explore museums
and art galleries

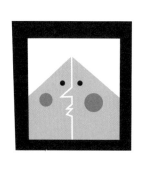

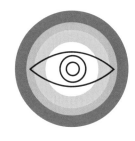

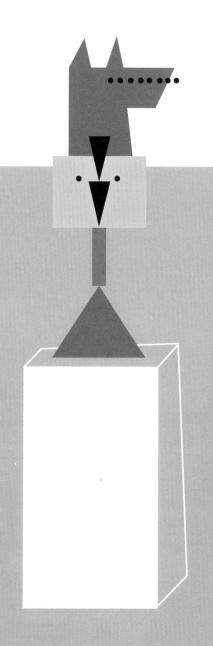

where there are things that
are beautiful and full of history.

At the zoo, you can see amazing animals
that don't come from the city

but can teach us about nature.

People in the city have many different jobs.

Which ones do you know?

People also like to do fun things.

What fun things do you like to do?

Cities grow and change all the time

but people get
used to changes
very quickly.

Many cities are built by the water.

Boats can be used for transportation,
for fun, or even to live on.

People in the city like to shop.

They can visit shopping malls
with lots of different stores in one place.

Some people prefer smaller stores on the street

where they can buy things
that are special and unique.

There are also busy,
bustling markets

full of fresh and
colorful produce.

In the evening, the city comes alive with beautiful colors and music.

At night, some parts of the city are fast asleep.

But not everyone
sleeps at night.
Who is still awake?

At sunrise, everything wakes up again
to start another busy day in the city.

Dominika Lipniewska is a Polish illustrator and designer. A graduate of Central Saint Martins College of Art and Design and Cambridge School of Art in the UK, she has published several books. Dominika lives and works in London, which she considers an endless source of inspiration.

www.dolidomino.com

First published 2019 by Button Books, an imprint of Guild of Master Craftsman Publications Ltd, Castle Place, 166 High Street, Lewes, East Sussex BN7 1XU. Illustrations © Dominika Lipniewska, 2019. Copyright in the Work © GMC Publications Ltd, 2019. ISBN 978 1 78708 031 7. Distributed by Publishers Group West in the United States. All rights reserved. The right of Dominika Lipniewska to be identified as the author of this work has been asserted in accordance with the Copyright, Designs and Patents Act 1988, sections 77 and 78. No part of this publication may be reproduced, stored in a retrieval system, or transmitted in any form or by any means without the prior permission of the publisher and copyright owner. This book is sold subject to the condition that all designs are copyright and are not for commercial reproduction without the permission of the designer and copyright owner. While every effort has been made to obtain permission from the copyright holders for all material used in this book, the publishers will be pleased to hear from anyone who has not been appropriately acknowledged and to make the correction in future reprints. The publishers and author can accept no legal responsibility for any consequences arising from the application of information, advice, or instructions given in this publication. A catalog record for this book is available from the British Library. Publisher: Jonathan Bailey, Production: Jim Bulley, Jo Pallett, Senior Project Editor: Virginia Brehaut, Managing Art Editor: Gilda Pacitti. Color origination by GMC Reprographics. Printed and bound in China.

Button
Books

For more on Button Books, contact:
GMC Publications Ltd., Castle Place, 166 High Street, Lewes, East Sussex, BN7 1XU, United Kingdom.
Tel +44 (0)1273 488005
www.buttonbooks.co.uk

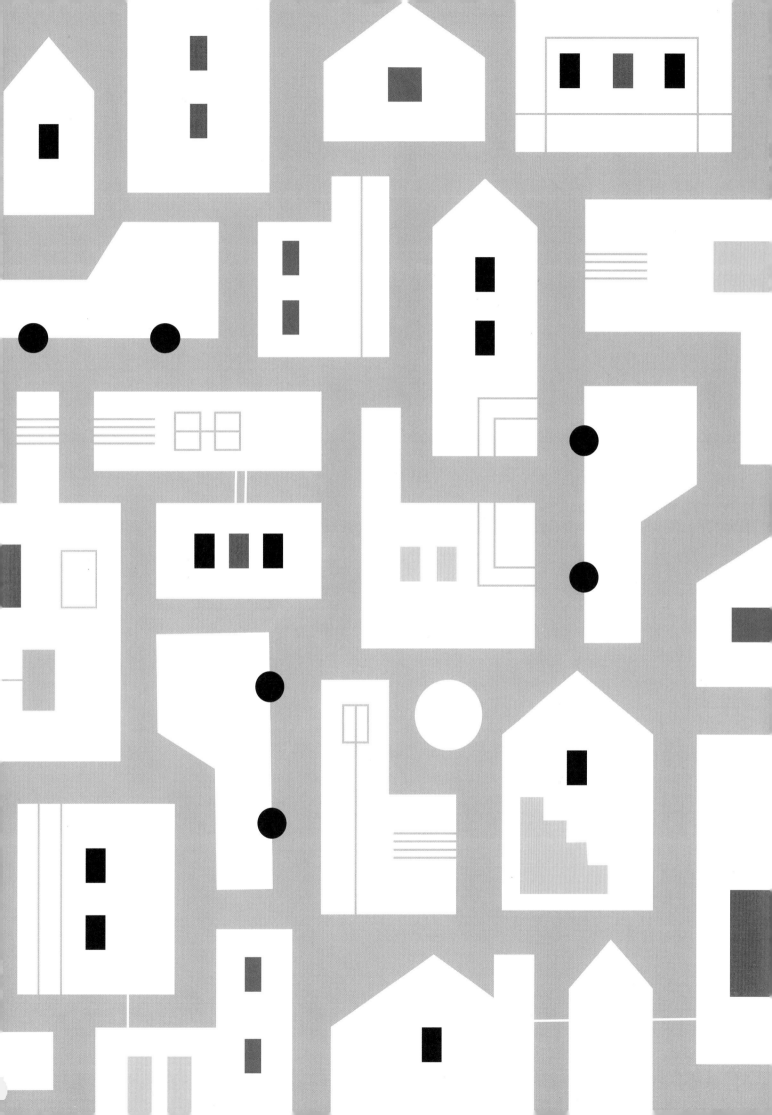

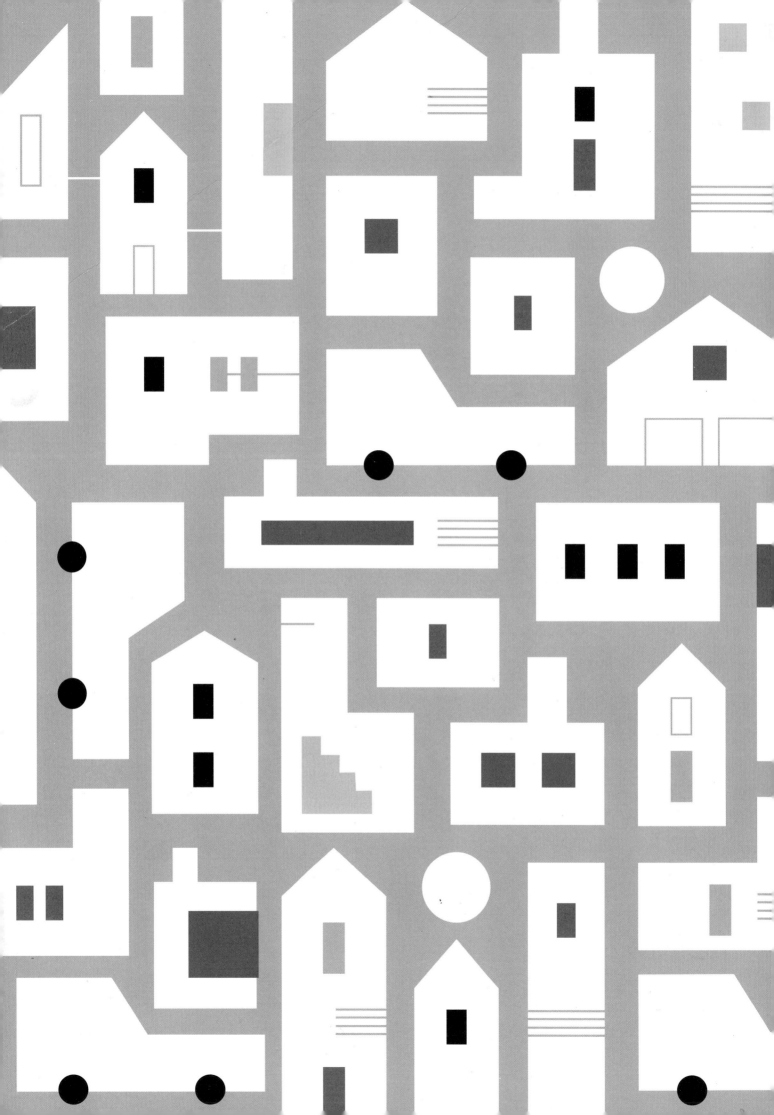